PREPARE TO
PROSPER

PREPARE TO PROSPER

*Moving from
the Land of Lack
to the Land
of Plenty*

JOYCE MEYER

WARNER
Faith®

NEW YORK   BOSTON   NASHVILLE

Unless otherwise indicated, all Scripture quotations are taken from *The Amplified Bible* (AMP). *Old Testament* copyright © 1965, 1987 by The Zondervan Corporation, Grand Rapids, Michigan. *New Testament* copyright © 1954, 1958, 1987 by The Lockman Foundation. Used by permission.

Scripture quotations marked (KJV) are taken from the *King James Version* of the Bible.

Warner Books Edition
Copyright © 1997 by Joyce Meyer
Life In The Word, Inc.
P.O. Box 655
Fenton, Missouri 63026
All rights reserved.

Warner Faith

Time Warner Book Group
1271 Avenue of the Americas, New York, NY 10020
Visit our Web site at www.twbookmark.com.

Warner Faith® and the Warner Faith logo are trademarks of Time Warner Book Group Inc.

Printed in the United States of America

First Warner Faith Edition: February 2003

10 9 8 7 6 5 4

ISBN: 0-446-69145-3

LCCN: 2002115550

CONTENTS

INTRODUCTION

For the Lord your God is bringing you
into a good land, a land of brooks of
water, of fountains and springs,
flowing forth in valleys and hills;

A land of wheat and barley, and vines
and fig trees and pomegranates, a land
of olive trees and honey;

A land in which you shall eat food
without shortage and lack nothing in
it; a land whose stones are iron and
out of whose hills you can dig copper.

DEUTERONOMY 8:7,9

$\mathcal{M}$any people believe and act upon the biblical principles of tithing and giving offerings, yet they never seem to be able to leave what I call the "land of even." Though their basic needs are met, they feel as though they're living from paycheck to paycheck.

The Word of God clearly teaches that God desires for us to live in the "land of plenty." God brought the Israelites out of the land of lack, through the land of even and into the land of plenty.

It was God's will for every one of the Israelites to live in abundance. However, the sad fact is only a handful of those who came out of Egypt actually crossed over the Jordan and lived in the land of promise—the land of plenty.

Precisely the same situation appears in every generation—a few enter into the best God has provided for them through Jesus Christ, while the majority barely get by. They struggle and struggle, seeing a better land but remaining confused as to why they cannot take up residence there.

This book focuses on one of the main reasons for that failure to "enter in." There are a variety of roadblocks to the abundant life. But in this book, I center in on a major one about which, I believe, we all need to be encouraged.

I pray your prosperity will radically increase as a result of reading this book and applying the principles you have read.

1

SOW YOUR SEED—
THEN WHAT?

While the earth remains, seedtime
and harvest . . . shall not cease.

GENESIS 8:22

*A*ny person desiring a harvest knows he must first plant seed. *Without seedtime, there can never be a harvest*. This is a spiritual, as well as a natural, law. Therefore, in ministering we often teach people how to prosper in every realm through this God-established principle of sowing and reaping.

This book, however, does not focus on sowing seed, but on how to water the seed already sown. God has been showing me that many people sow without ever enjoying the harvest He would love to give them because they are not properly caring for seed sown.

Proper seed
planted in proper ground
under proper conditions
produces a prosperous harvest!

The principle I share in this book is simple, but I have sensed an urgency to put it in writing. For many people this principle may be a "missing link" to prosperity.

The Lord spoke to my heart, "Joyce, you need to have a special season of watering the seed you have sown. This is preparation for a new level of prosperity." He quickly began placing specific Scriptures on my heart which helped me understand what He wanted me to do and why.

We are taught to sow our seed, but what comes after that? The seed requires proper care. It will grow and produce a harvest only under proper conditions.

2

WATER YOUR SEED

For as the rain and snow come down
from the heavens, and return not there
again, but water the earth and make it
bring forth and sprout, that it may give
seed to the sower and bread to the eater,

So shall My word be that goes forth
out of My mouth: it shall not return to
Me void [without producing any effect,
useless], but it shall accomplish that
which I please and purpose, and it shall
prosper in the thing for which I sent it.

ISAIAH 55:10,11

A careful study of the above Scripture verses reveals a biblical principle that operates in both the natural and spiritual realms. Rain and snow (water) come down and water the seeds in the earth to *make* it bring forth a harvest.

God's Word operates in the same way. When it is spoken out in faith, the Word does not return void (does not return without accomplishing something), but prospers whatever it is spoken over. The Word of God spoken out in faith waters the seed. Ephesians 5:26 refers to the washing of water with the Word.

Speaking God's Word over the financial seed we have sown will cause that seed to prosper (grow) and bring forth a harvest. Just as natural seed will not produce a harvest without being regularly watered, neither will spiritual seed.

3

~~~

DON'T CURSE YOUR SEED

$\mathcal{A}$t times believers may speak in agreement with
what they see happening around them instead of
speaking in agreement with what God has promised in the Bible. They are cursing their seed
without realizing what they are doing! <u>Continu-
ing to speak in line with God's promises</u> while the
<u>seed is growing is important</u> to bringing us out of
the "land of even" into the abundant harvest.

Verses 10 and 11 of Malachi chapter 3, a
chapter well-known for its teaching on tithing
and giving, describe the blessings God tells Israel
tithing will bring: God will rebuke the devourer

for the tither's sake! The fruit of their ground will not be destroyed and all nations will call them happy and blessed. (Vv. 11,12.) By obeying God's directions, rather than following the world's system, they would be blessed.

Chapter 3 also describes God's instruction to Israel of how to be cursed! Verse 8 states that withholding tithes and offerings robs God. God addresses Israel in verse 9: **You are cursed with the curse, for you are robbing Me, even this whole nation** (v. 9). The Lord wanted the people to bring their tithes to the storehouse to prove Him. When they brought tithes in obedience to His system, He would pour them out a blessing so big, there would not be room to contain it.

God was trying to get the people to follow His system so that He could bless them. Instead of expressing their faith in Him through their words, Malachi says the people's words had been strong and hard against God:

Your words have been strong and hard
against Me, says the Lord. Yet you say,
What have we spoken against You?

MALACHI 3:13

Malachi 3:14,15 says:

You have said, It is useless to serve
God, and what profit is it if we keep
His ordinances and walk gloomily
and as if in mourning apparel before
the Lord of hosts?

And now we consider the proud
and arrogant to be happy and
favored; evildoers are exalted and
prosper; yes, and when they test
God, they escape [unpunished].

I have heard people say (and I have even
said this myself during times of frustration),
"What good is it doing me to give all the time?

Every time I turn around, we are having financial trouble. Even unbelievers seem to do better financially than I do."

I remember a woman who worked for me being confused because her unbelieving, stingy brother always had more money than she and her husband, who were believers trying to operate in the principles of giving.

Psalm 37:1 teaches us not to fret over evildoers, nor to be envious of them. Sometimes it looks as if worldly people have more material things than those who are trying to serve God, but we are promised in the end we will inherit the earth. (v. 11.) As it is said, "It isn't over until it's over."

Worldly people sometimes obtain things through means that are unacceptable according to God's Word by compromising, cheating, people-pleasing and doing all sorts of other things that displease God.

These methods, however, produce no peace or joy. They may temporarily produce things, but the effectiveness of these methods usually does not last forever.

The child of God seems to go through a testing period—a period of doing what is right even though he doesn't seem to be getting the right results. As he persists in faith, breakthroughs start happening. He eventually ends up with a harvest, only his harvest is accompanied by peace and joy! It has come to him by righteous means—not unrighteous ones.

What is said during these testing times is very important. Proverbs 18:21 states:

Death and life are in the power of the tongue, and they who indulge in it shall eat the fruit of it [for death or life].

To begin blurting out negative statements from emotion is extremely unfruitful. Speaking out of our emotions is not the right thing to do. Our emotions usually don't do well in times of testing. As we mature in Christ, we learn to control both the emotions and the mouth.

You and I can speak death or life to our seed. After we give—after our seed has been planted—we should speak life to it. Water that seed with the Word of God. Don't curse it by speaking negative things.

Speaking about our financial future or about the principles of giving in a negative way ministers death to the seed we have just planted. The result is this: it will not mature and bring forth an abundant harvest in our lives.

Speaking positively when everything seems to be going wrong is especially challenging. I can remember becoming very upset in the beginning days of our Spirit-led walk with God when Dave would tell me we needed to buy new tires or to repair the lawn mower—or, even worse, replace it!

The refrigerator would break down, or the washing machine would quit rinsing the clothes properly. It seemed as though it was always something, and Satan used it to confuse me. "We are giving!" I would say, "And I do not understand why these things keep happening."

I had not learned the power of praise—of refusing to complain no matter what the circumstances appear to be. I had not learned to call those things that are not as if they are. (Romans 4:17.)

I spoke emotionally. I was upset, and I said things that were negative. I felt negative, so I spoke negatively! Therefore, we stayed in the land of even. We barely survived from paycheck to paycheck, needing a miracle every month to make ends meet. But, praise God, He sticks with us, and by His Spirit, He teaches us how we can be blessed.

I learned the dangers of complaining. I found 1 Corinthians 10:10 which says, Nor discontentedly complain as some of them did—and were put out of the way entirely by the destroyer (death). When the Israelites complained and murmured, snakes came into the camp and bit them Many people died.

I don't mean physical death will result from complaining, but I do believe there is a principle here which we need to give close attention. Complaining ministers death. It steals our joy, our peace and our progress. If people complain about what they already have, why should God give them any more to complain about? Complaining is a sign of immaturity—a sign of carnality.

Complaining is a normal function of the flesh—we may always have to resist it. But as we choose to walk in the Spirit, there is no room for it. The normal atmosphere for those walking in the Spirit is one of praise and thanksgiving.

Don't kill your seed with your words! Water the seed you have sown by speaking life to it. Call those things that are not (the negative things you see around you) as if they are (lining up with God's promises to you in His Word). Give God praise and thanksgiving. He will grow the seed you have sown into an abundant harvest to take you into the land of plenty!

4

~※~

PLANT MORE SEEDS
TO MEET MORE NEEDS

And God is able to make all grace (every
favor and earthly blessing) come to you
in abundance, so that you may always
and under all circumstances and
whatever the need be self-sufficient
[possessing enough to require no aid
or support and furnished in abundance
for every good work and charitable
donation].

2 CORINTHIANS 9:8

$\mathcal{M}$y husband, Dave, and I have a desire to meet more needs, as I am sure you do also. You and I cannot meet more needs without a greater harvest in our lives. *To have more output, we must have more income.* God desires to meet our own needs abundantly and also provide enough that we may help others and meet their needs. *It is time to water your seeds so that you can eventually meet more needs!*

The ability to meet more and more needs occurs in levels or degrees. The Lord gives us a little to take care of and <u>as we are faithful over</u> it, He gives increase and allows us to be stewards over more. (See Matthew 25:23.) Matthew 25 shares a parable of the talents. A man gave three of his servants talents according to their individual abilities then traveled to a distant country. Two of the three servants invested their talents and increased. The fearful third servant hid his in the ground.

When the master returned for an accounting, he rebuked the servant who had acted in fear and gave that servant's talent to one of the servants who had invested and increased his talents. The fearful servant lost even the one talent he had. The two who invested and increased were honored and brought into a new level of prosperity and responsibility.

Matthew 25:23 says: His master said to him, Well done, you upright (honorable, admirable) and faithful servant! You have been faithful and trustworthy over a little; I will put you in charge of much. Enter into and share the joy (the delight, the blessedness) which your master enjoys.

As I look back to the place I began when I initially learned these principles, I am amazed at how far God has brought Dave and me in being blessed *and* being a blessing. You and I should never desire only blessing for ourselves. God spoke a promise to Abram recorded in Genesis 12:2: And I will make of you a great nation, and I will bless you [with abundant increase of favors] and make your name famous and distinguished, and you will be a blessing [dispensing good to others].

Actually both areas progress simultaneously. As we bless others (sow seeds), we are blessed (reap a harvest). We see clearly that the principles of seedtime and harvest do remain today.

Dave and I know the principles of sowing and reaping. We know the meaning of Acts 20:35: It is more blessed to give than to receive (KJV).

Giving brings tremendous joy into our lives. It is enjoyable to fill our minds with ways to bless others. My giving has become one of my highest priorities in life—God is first, my family is second and my giving is third.

I spent many frustrating years struggling, trying to change myself and all my circumstances. I must admit I was unhappy until I discovered the secret of joyful living—it is joyful giving! I took my mind off myself and purposely turned my thoughts to how I could be a blessing to someone else.

If you have not discovered this secret of joyful living, purposely think of ways to be a blessing to others with what God has made available to you. Follow through and become a radical giver of your time, talents, money and prayers. In fact, give your entire life to God for His service, and be determined to look for ways to bless others.

As we joyfully give, we are sowing seed that will eventually produce a harvest of blessings in every realm of our lives: spiritual, physical, financial, social and mental. Sowing seed is the basis upon which to believe God for progress.

Dave and I have been tithing since we were married in 1967. We attended a church that taught tithing, and we experienced a protection on our lives as a result of obeying the Word in this area. But we still lived in what I refer to as "the land of even."

As we began seriously studying and practicing the Word of God, we started stepping out into new levels of giving. When God recently spoke to me saying, "I want you to have a season of watering the seed you have sown, because I want to bring you into a new level of prosperity," I was excited. I know that God does promote people, and He does it in levels. Usually, everything does not come all at once.

I knew it was important for me to listen and grasp what He was trying to show me. You may be at the same place right now I was. God desires to promote you into new levels of prosperity, and He wants you to begin to water the seeds you have sown. *God wants you to prepare to prosper!*

5

---⟿⟿⟊⟿---

THE PRACTICAL SIDE
OF WATERING YOUR SEED

We have seen we need to stay positive, even in the challenging times that test us. You and I must resist the temptation to speak negatively even when we feel negative. But we also need to go the extra mile to speak positive things *on purpose* and confess Scriptures pertaining to giving over our seed.

This is what God showed me to do: Every day—perhaps even several times a day—quote Bible verses aloud that pertain to prosperity. Remember, it is the Word that waters the seed.

I made a list of these Scriptures. Many I already knew; others I committed to memory or read from either a note pad or the Bible.

In looking up the Scriptures and writing them down, I had to do a little homework. I have done your homework for you and provided you with a list of good "watering Scriptures" to use in watering your seed. You will find them at the back of this book.

Soon after I began to practice what God had spoken to me, I saw results. I was confessing an increased harvest for both the ministry and our personal finances. Within two weeks I saw both areas increase in blessings.

Several large offerings came into the ministry, and I noticed over a period of several weeks the general finances of the ministry increased overall.

I was personally blessed with some money and even experienced an increase in gifts being given to me. I was careful to <u>remember to give</u> <u>more also</u>. I urge you to <u>always remember to be</u> a <u>blessing</u>. Don't ever be foolish enough to eat your seed. <u>Anytime your harvest comes in</u> or <u>increases, set aside seed to sow</u>. <u>The idea is</u> to <u>plant and water until you see harvest</u>, then keep <u>planting and watering *during* harvest</u>.

<u>As one harvest runs out, another will</u> be <u>coming</u> in. <u>You will eventually move into an area</u> <u>of living in harvest</u>. You will be living in the "land of plenty," the equivalent of the Promised Land, referred to in the Bible!

The principle of confessing the Word of God is simple—so simple, in fact, it could be overlooked. I learned the power of confession many years ago. *Vine's Complete Expository Dictionary of Old and New Testament Words* defines the word <u>"confess"</u> in the Greek as <u>*homologeo*</u> which means "to speak the same thing"; "to assent, accord, agree with"; "to confess, declare, admit"; "to declare openly by way of speaking out freely, such confession being the effect of deep conviction of facts."[1]

We must be in agreement with God if we desire for His will to manifest in our lives. Being in agreement with Him includes speaking in agreement with Him. God wants to bless us even more than we can imagine.

Joshua 1:8 says: This Book of the Law shall not depart out of your mouth, but you shall meditate on it day and night, that you may observe and do according to all that is written in it. For then you shall make your way prosperous, and then you shall deal wisely and have good success.

I sincerely believe if you will plant your seed and diligently water it with the Word, you will see a greater harvest manifested in your life. James 5:7 reminds us, So be patient, brethren, [as you wait] till the coming of the Lord. See how the farmer waits expectantly for the precious harvest from the land. [See how] he keeps up his patient [vigil] over it until it receives the early and late rains.

The farmer maintains a specific routine in caring for the seed he has planted until his harvest comes. He is patient about it. He does not expect to plant the seed and have it produce a harvest the next day. Nor does he plant it, walk away from it, and expect to do nothing else to provide for its care. He continues to water it, pulls weeds and makes sure it gets plenty of sunshine.

First Corinthians 3:6 says, I planted, Apollos watered, but God [all the while] was making it grow and [He] gave the increase.

Paul was talking about the seed of God's Word planted in the hearts of the people, but the principle is the same. Paul planted the Word in them, Apollos watered it and God gave increase. We can never have increase without planting seed, and neither can we have increase without watering the seed that has been planted.

1. W. E. Vine, Merrill F. Unger, William White, Jr., "New Testament Section," in *Vine's Complete Expository Dictionary of Old and New Testament Words* (Nashville: Thomas Nelson, Inc., 1984), p. 120, s.v. "CONFESS."

Scriptures That Will Water Your Seed

I believe confessing these Scriptures aloud, mixed with faith, will increase your harvest. Meditate on them as Joshua 1:8 teaches. They will become part of your life, and you will prosper and have good success.

> Then Isaac sowed seed in that land and received in the same year a hundred times as much as he had planted, and the Lord favored him with blessings.

And the man became great and gained more and more until he became very wealthy and distinguished . . . and the Philistines envied him.

GENESIS 26:12–14

And I will make My covenant (solemn pledge) between Me and you and will multiply you exceedingly.

GENESIS 17:2

~ See, I have set before you today life and good, death and evil, in that I command you today to love the Lord your God, to walk in His ways, and to keep His commandments, His statutes, and His judgments, that you may live and multiply; and the Lord your God will bless you in the land which you go to possess.

DEUTERONOMY 30:15,16 NKJV

For the Lord God is a sun and shield:
the Lord will give grace and glory: no
good thing will he withhold from
them that walk uprightly.

PSALM 84:11 KJV

Blessed shall you be when you come
in and blessed shall you be when you
go out.

The Lord shall command the blessing
upon you in your storehouse and in
all that you undertake. And He will
bless you in the land which the Lord
your God gives you.

And the Lord shall make you have a
surplus of prosperity, through the fruit
of your body, of your livestock, and of
your ground, in the land which the
Lord swore to your fathers to give you.

The Lord shall open to you His good treasury, the heavens, to give the rain of your land in its season and to bless all the work of your hands; and you shall lend to many nations, but you shall not borrow.

And the Lord shall make you the head, and not the tail; and you shall be above only, and you shall not be beneath, if you heed the commandments of the Lord your God which I command you this day and are watchful to do them.

DEUTERONOMY 28:6,8,11–13

Trust in the Lord instead. Be kind and good to others; then you will live safely here in the land and prosper, feeding in safety.

PSALM 37:3 TLB

The generous man will be prosperous,
And he who waters will himself be
watered.

PROVERBS 11:25 NASB

The merciful, kind, and generous man
benefits himself [for his deeds return
to bless him], but he who is cruel and
callous [to the wants of others] brings
on himself retribution.

PROVERBS 11:17

He who gives to the poor will not
want, but he who hides his eyes [from
their want] will have many a curse.

PROVERBS 28:27

Note: I would say now, "I have given to the
poor. I care about them. Therefore I am blessed."

To the reader: You, of course, may turn these
Scriptures into very personal confessions based
upon your individual giving.

Cast your bread upon the waters, for after many days you will find it again.

ECCLESIASTES 11:1 NIV

Save now, we beseech You, O Lord; send now prosperity, O Lord, we beseech You, and give to us success!

PSALM 118:25

Let those who favor my righteous cause and have pleasure in my uprightness shout for joy and be glad and say continually, Let the Lord be magnified, Who takes pleasure in the prosperity of His servant.

PSALM 35:27

- The wicked borrow and pay not again [for they may be unable], but the [uncompromisingly] righteous deal kindly and give [for they are able].

PSALM 37:21

I have been young and now am old,
yet have I not seen the [uncompromis-
ingly] righteous forsaken or their seed
begging bread.

All day long they are merciful and deal
graciously; they lend, and their
offspring are blessed.

PSALM 37:25,26

My confession is, "I AM ABLE TO GIVE!"

May the Lord give you increase more
and more, you and your children.

May you be blessed of the Lord, Who
made heaven and earth!

PSALM 115:14,15

The blessing of the Lord brings
wealth, and he adds no trouble to it.

PROVERBS 10:22 NIV

⌐ But as it is written, Eye hath not seen,
nor ear heard, neither have entered
into the heart of man, the things
which God hath prepared for them
that love him.

1 CORINTHIANS 2:9 KJV

Blessed is the man who does not walk
in the counsel of the wicked or stand
in the way of sinners or sit in the seat
of mockers.

But his delight is in the law of the
Lord, and on his law he meditates day
and night.

He is like a tree planted by streams of
water, which yields its fruit in season
and whose leaf does not wither. Whatever he does prospers.

PSALM 1:1–3 NIV

Honor the Lord with your possessions,

And with the first fruits of all your increase;

So your barns will be filled with plenty, And your vats will overflow with new wine.

PROVERBS 3:9,10 NKJV

If you are willing and obedient, you shall eat the good of the land.

ISAIAH 1:19

This Book of the Law shall not depart from your mouth, but you shall meditate in it day and night, that you may observe to do according to all that is written in it. For then you will make your way prosperous, and then you will have good success.

JOSHUA 1:8 NKJV

No one's ever seen or heard anything like this,

Never so much as imagined anything
quite like it—

What God has arranged for those who
love him.

1 CORINTHIANS 2:9 MESSAGE

Now to Him Who, by (in consequence
of) the [action of His] power that is at
work within us, is able to [carry out
His purpose and] do super-abundantly,
far over and above all that we [dare]
ask or think [infinitely beyond our
highest prayers, desires, thoughts,
hopes, or dreams].

EPHESIANS 3:20

Give, and it shall be given unto you;
good measure, pressed down, and
shaken together, and running over,
shall men give into your bosom. For
with the same measure that ye mete

42

withal it shall be measured to you
again.

LUKE 6:38 KJV

Note: I turn these Scriptures into first person
confessions when I quote them aloud over my
seed. For example, I would say this one like this:

*I have given, and it is given unto me, good
measure, pressed down and shaken
together, and running over, shall men give
into my bosom. For with the same measure
that I have meted out to others, it shall be
measured to me again.*

And my God will liberally supply (fill
to the full) your every need according
to His riches in glory in Christ Jesus.

PHILIPPIANS 4:19

Now as you abound and excel and are
at the front in everything—in faith, in

43

expressing yourselves, in knowledge,
in all zeal, and in your love for us—
[see to it that you come to the front
now and] abound and excel in this
gracious work [of almsgiving] also.

2 CORINTHIANS 8:7

My confession is, "I EXCEL IN ALMSGIVING!"

[Remember] this: he who sows
sparingly and grudgingly will also reap
sparingly and grudgingly, and he who
sows generously [that blessings may
come to someone] will also reap
generously and with blessings.

Let each one [give] as he has made up
his own mind and purposed in his
heart, not reluctantly or sorrowfully or
under compulsion, for God loves (He
takes pleasure in, prizes above other

things, and is unwilling to abandon or
to do without) a cheerful (joyous,
"prompt to do it") giver [whose heart
is in his giving].

And God is able to make all grace
(every favor and earthly blessing)
come to you in abundance, so that
you may always and under all
circumstances and whatever the need
be self-sufficient [possessing enough
to require no aid or support and
furnished in abundance for every good
work and charitable donation].

As it is written, He [the benevolent
person] scatters abroad; He gives to
the poor; His deeds of justice and
goodness and kindness and benevo-
lence will go on and endure forever!

2 CORINTHIANS 9:6–11

And God is able to make all grace abound to you, that always having all sufficiency in everything, you may have an abundance for every good deed.

2 CORINTHIANS 9:8 NASB

But seek first the kingdom of God and His righteousness, and all these things shall be added to you.

MATTHEW 6:33 NKJV

Beloved, I pray that you may prosper in every way and [that your body] may keep well, even as [I know] your soul keeps well and prospers.

3 JOHN 1:2

~ . . . I pray for good fortune in everything you do, and for your good health—that your everyday affairs prosper, as well as your soul!

3 JOHN 1:2 MESSAGE

I, even I, have spoken; yea, I have
called him: I have brought him, and
he shall make his way prosperous . . .

Thus saith the Lord, thy Redeemer,
the Holy One of Israel; I am the Lord
thy God which teacheth thee to profit,
which leadeth thee by the way that
thou shouldest go.

ISAIAH 48:15,17 KJV

Behold, My Servant shall deal wisely
and shall prosper; He shall be exalted
and extolled and shall stand very high.
(This Scripture is referring to Jesus, but
remember we are joint-heirs with Him.)

ISAIAH 52:13

He set himself to seek God in the days
of Zechariah, who instructed him in
the things of God; and as long as he

sought (inquired of, yearned for) the
Lord, God made him prosper.

2 CHRONICLES 26:5

For you are becoming progressively
acquainted with and recognizing more
strongly and clearly the grace of our
Lord Jesus Christ (His kindness, His
gracious generosity, His undeserved
favor and spiritual blessing), [in] that
though He was [so very] rich, yet for
your sakes He became [so very] poor,
in order that by His poverty you might
become enriched (abundantly
supplied).

2 CORINTHIANS 8:9

The earth has yielded its harvest [in
evidence of God's approval]; God,
even our own God, will bless us.

PSALM 67:6

Let them shout for joy and be glad,
Who favor my righteous cause;
And let them say continually,
"Let the Lord be magnified,
Who has pleasure in the prosperity of
His servant."

PSALM 35:27 NKJV

But you shall [earnestly] remember
the Lord your God, for it is He Who
gives you power to get wealth, that He
may establish His covenant which He
swore to your fathers, as it is this day.

DEUTERONOMY 8:18

Therefore keep the words of this covenant, and do them, that you may
prosper in all that you do.

DEUTERONOMY 29:9 NKJV

. . . my cup runneth over.

PSALM 23:5 KJV

Bring ye all the tithes into the
storehouse, that there may be meat in
mine house, and prove me now
herewith, saith the Lord of hosts, if I
will not open you the windows of
heaven, and pour you out a blessing,
that there shall not be room enough to
receive it.

And I will rebuke the devourer for
your sakes, and he shall not destroy
the fruits of your ground; neither shall
your vine cast her fruit before the time
in the field, saith the Lord of hosts.

And all nations shall call you blessed:
for ye shall be a delightsome land, saith
the Lord of hosts.

MALACHI 3:10–12 KJV

And the Lord your God will make you
abundantly prosperous in every work

of your hand, in the fruit of your body, of your cattle, of your land, for good; for the Lord will again delight in prospering you, as He took delight in your fathers.

DEUTERONOMY 30:9

The thief comes only in order to steal and kill and destroy. I came that they may have and enjoy life, and have it in abundance (to the full, till it over-flows).

JOHN 10:10

The eyes of the Lord are toward the [uncompromisingly] righteous and His ears are open to their cry.

PSALM 34:15

They spend their days in prosperity. . . .

JOB 21:13

Prosperity and welfare are in his house,
and his righteousness endures forever.

PSALM 112:3

. . . but prosperity is the reward of the
righteous.

PROVERBS 13:21 NIV

. . . but he who trusts in the Lord will
prosper.

PROVERBS 28:25 NIV

Saying, Blessing I certainly will bless
you and multiplying I will multiply you.

HEBREWS 6:14

And without faith it is impossible to
please God, because anyone who
comes to him must believe that he
exists and that he *rewards* those who
earnestly seek him.

HEBREWS 11:6 NIV

* * *

Be sure you plant your seed into good ground. The Bible says in Deuteronomy 26:12–14 we should not give our tithe to the dead. After planting, expect to be blessed and say so. Confess frequently:

I am blessed, and I am a blessing.
Everything I lay my hand to prospers and succeeds.
I am blessed when I come in and blessed when I go out.
I have favor everywhere I go.
God is multiplying me.
I seek first the kingdom of God and He adds all other things that I need.
I love to give.
I always have plenty of seed to sow and bread to eat.
My cup runs over.

Goodness and mercy follow me all the days of my life.
I always have more than enough.

By confessing these and other Scriptures you find and by making these personal confessions, you will build an image of prosperity in your spirit. Your spirit wants to work for you, but it can only produce what you put in it.

When your spirit, mind, and mouth line up in agreement with God, you are undefeatable! As you develop a prosperous image, and keep an expectant attitude toward prosperity, you will begin to reap a harvest in abundance.

NEVER EAT YOUR SEED! Each harvest produces seed to sow as well as bread to eat. Keep sowing, and you will eventually come to the place where you continually have a new harvest coming in.

Amos 9:13 says: Behold, the days are coming, says the Lord, that the plowman shall overtake the reaper, and the treader of grapes him who sows the seed; and the mountains shall drop sweet wine and all the hills shall melt [that is, everything heretofore barren and un-fruitful shall overflow with spiritual blessing].

I believe we have entered those days. Jesus is coming back soon. He is returning for a glori-ous Church—not a poor, pathetic, broken-down Church. I have written this book to help you pre-pare to prosper. I know that prosperity is God's will for each person.

Prosperity is not just money, but blessing in *every* realm. *Sow your seed, water it with the Word of God, expect a harvest and prepare to prosper!*

References

Scripture quotations marked (NIV) are taken from the *Holy Bible, New International Version®*. NIV®. Copyright © 1973, 1978, 1984 by International Bible Society. Used by permission of Zondervan Publishing House. All rights reserved.

Scripture quotations marked (KJV) are taken frm the *King James Version* of the Bible.

Scripture quotations marked (TLB) are taken from *The Living Bible* © 1971. Used by permission of Tyndale House Publishers, Inc. Wheaton, Illinois 60189. All rights reserved.

Scripture quotations marked (MESSAGE) are taken from *The Message: New Testament With Psalms and Proverbs* by Eugene H. Peterson.

ABOUT THE AUTHOR

JOYCE MEYER has been teaching the Word of God since 1976 and in full-time ministry since 1980. She is the bestselling author of more than sixty inspirational books, including *In Pursuit of Peace, How to Hear from God, Knowing God Intimately*, and *Battlefield of the Mind*. She has also released thousands of teaching cassettes and a complete video library. Joyce's *Enjoying Everyday Life* radio and television programs are broadcast around the world, and she travels extensively conducting conferences. Joyce and her husband, Dave, are the parents of four grown children and make their home in St. Louis, Missouri.

To contact the author write:

Joyce Meyer Ministries
P. O. Box 655
Fenton, Missouri 63026
or call: (636) 349-0303

Internet Address: www.joycemeyer.org

Please include your testimony or help received from this book when you write. Your prayer requests are welcome.

To contact the author
in Canada, please write:
Joyce Meyer Ministries Canada, Inc.
Lambeth Box 1300
London, ON N6P 1T5
or call: (636) 349-0303

In Australia, please write:
Joyce Meyer Ministries-Australia
Locked Bag 77
Mansfield Delivery Centre
Queensland 4122
or call: (07) 3349 1200

In England, please write:
Joyce Meyer Ministries
P. O. Box 1549
Windsor
SL4 1GT

Or call: (0) 1753 831102

Joyce Meyer Titles

Me and My Big Mouth!
Me and My Big Mouth! Study Guide
Prepare to Prosper
Do It Afraid!
Expect a Move of God in Your Life...Suddenly!
Enjoying Where You Are on the Way to
Where You Are Going
The Most Important Decision You Will Ever Make
When, God, When?
Why, God, Why?
The Word, the Name, the Blood
Battlefield of the Mind
Battlefield of the Mind Study Guide
Tell Them I Love Them
Peace
The Root of Rejection
If Not for the Grace of God
If Not for the Grace of God Study Guide

JOYCE MEYER SPANISH TITLES
Las Siete Cosas Que Te Roban el Gozo
(Seven Things That Steal Your Joy)
Empezando Tu Día Bien (Starting Your Day Right)

BY DAVE MEYER
Life Lines

①

412 222 5215

Bus # 2182